PIANO TUTOR

WISE PUBLICATIONS
PART OF THE MUSIC SALES GROUP
LONDON / NEW YORK / PARIS / SYDNEY / COPENHAGEN / BERLIN / MADRID / TOKYO

ALL TITLES CONTAIN BACKGROUND NOTES FOR EACH SONG PLUS
PLAYING TIPS AND HINTS.

PUBLISHED BY
WISE PUBLICATIONS
14-15 BERNERS STREET, LONDON, W1T 3LJ, UK.

EXCLUSIVE DISTRIBUTORS:
MUSIC SALES LIMITED
DISTRIBUTION CENTRE, NEWMARKET ROAD, BURY ST EDMUNDS,
SUFFOLK, IP33 3YB, UK.
MUSIC SALES PTY LIMITED
20 RESOLUTION DRIVE, CARINGBAH, NSW 2229, AUSTRALIA.

ORDER NO. AM996303
ISBN 978-1-84772-896-8
THIS BOOK © COPYRIGHT 2009 BY WISE PUBLICATIONS,
A DIVISION OF MUSIC SALES LIMITED.

BOOK DESIGNED BY CHLOE ALEXANDER.
EDITED BY FIONA BOLTON.

PRINTED IN THE EU.

YOUR GUARANTEE OF QUALITY
AS PUBLISHERS, WE STRIVE TO PRODUCE EVERY BOOK
TO THE HIGHEST COMMERCIAL STANDARDS. THE BOOK HAS
BEEN CAREFULLY DESIGNED TO MINIMISE AWKWARD PAGE
TURNS AND TO MAKE PLAYING FROM IT A REAL PLEASURE.
PARTICULAR CARE HAS BEEN GIVEN TO SPECIFYING ACID-FREE, NEUTRAL-
SIZED PAPER MADE FROM PULPS WHICH HAVE NOT BEEN ELEMENTAL
CHLORINE BLEACHED. THIS PULP IS FROM FARMED SUSTAINABLE FORESTS
AND WAS PRODUCED WITH SPECIAL REGARD FOR THE ENVIRONMENT.
THROUGHOUT, THE PRINTING AND BINDING HAVE BEEN PLANNED TO
ENSURE A STURDY, ATTRACTIVE PUBLICATION WHICH SHOULD GIVE YEARS
OF ENJOYMENT. IF YOUR COPY FAILS TO MEET OUR HIGH STANDARDS,
PLEASE INFORM US AND WE WILL GLADLY REPLACE IT.

WWW.MUSICSALES.COM

Welcome

Welcome to the REALLY EASY PIANO TUTOR, the really easy way to start playing your favourite songs and pieces on the piano. If you are someone who looks longingly at the piano and imagines all the music you would love to play, but all you can play is 'Chopsticks', this is the book for you!

We're going to look at the nuts and bolts of music, often referred to as the rudiments of music. We'll introduce notes, rhythms and various musical styles using lots of musical examples, so you'll be playing straightaway.

By the end of the book you'll be performing from written music using all of your fingers, ready to enjoy your favourite music from the REALLY EASY PIANO series whether it's pop, jazz, classical, show tunes or film themes.

Before we start looking at the music, let's make sure we have the correct **equipment** for the task, namely a piano or an electronic keyboard and a stool.

You may also want to purchase a mechanical or electrical metronome. Such a device makes repeated clicking sounds at a speed set by the user. It is particularly useful when practising as it can be used to mark rhythm and define a steady pace.

Are you sitting comfortably?

It is important to adopt the correct **position** when playing the piano in order to avoid injury and to ensure you can reach the keys easily.

Sit up, but don't tense. Your arms should be parallel to the floor and your fingers gently curved such that the pads of your fingers are lightly touching the keys.

Make sure your nails are kept short as long nails will restrict your ability to move up and down the keyboard freely.

A musical language

Written music is a language; a line of communication between the composer or songwriter
and the musician—that's you! It enables the composer to inform the musician what notes to play,
in what order to play them, how long each note should last, and much more besides.

With strange dots and unusual symbols scattered over the page, it might appear less like a language
and more like a secret code that is impossible to crack, but that's not the case. If you learn to read music,
just as you would learn a language, you'll soon understand how it works.

Let the translation begin!

Piano music uses two blocks of five horizontal lines called **staves**.

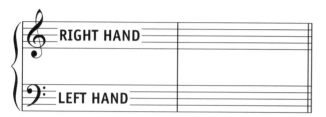

The top stave is primarily used for notes that are played
by the right hand; notes in the **treble clef**.

The lower stave is used predominantly for notes that are
played by the left hand; notes in the **bass clef**.

Each line, and each space between two lines, represents
a musical note. The first seven letters of the alphabet (A–G) are used to label these notes.

The notes most commonly played on the piano by the right and left hands are shown below.
Note that the last five notes in the bass clef are the same as the first five notes in the treble clef.

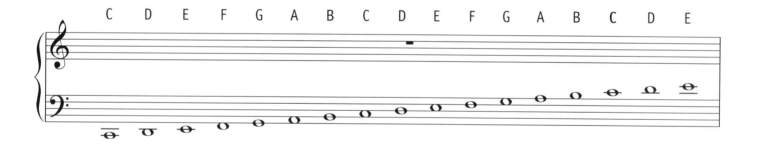

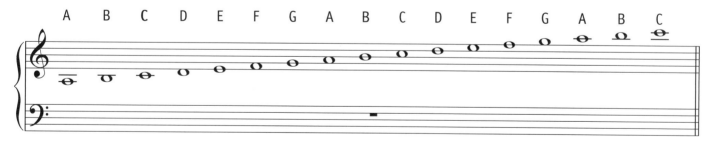

The first C in the treble clef is known as **middle C** because, as the name suggests, it is roughly in the
middle of the piano keyboard. The same note is also highlighted when it appears in the left hand.

As you can see, sometimes extra shorter lines, called **ledger lines**, need to be added in order to indicate
notes above or below the span of the stave.

Making the connection

The next step is to make the connection between the notes on the musical stave and the keys on the piano.

The piano keyboard is made up of a series of white and black keys with the lowest-sounding note to the left and the highest-sounding note to the right. If you look carefully you will notice a sequence comprising seven white keys and five black keys is repeated across its length.

The seven white keys are labelled with the first seven letters of the alphabet and correspond with the notes we looked at on the previous page.

Each series of 12 notes (seven white and five black) is called an **octave**.

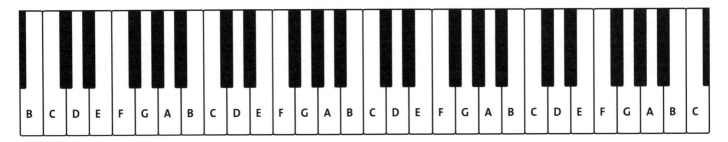

HAVE A GO!

Identify the notes below by writing the letter name of each in the gap above it.
Can you do this without referring to the guide on the previous page? Write in pencil so you can test yourself again and again. (Turn to page 47 for the solution.)

Then have a go at finding the notes on the piano. If you play the CD at the same time you'll be able to tell whether or not you're playing the correct notes. *TRACK 01*

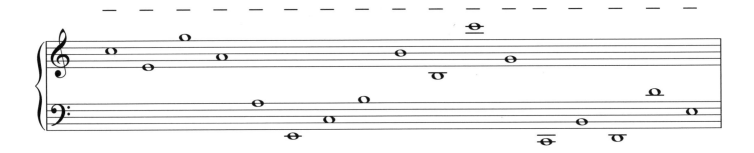

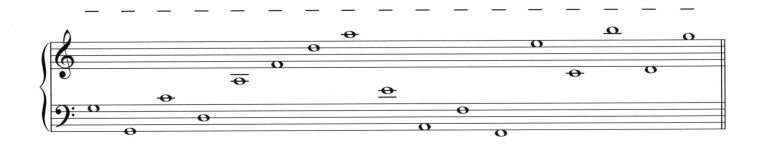

Rhythm

So far our musical language has told us what notes to play. Now we're ready to think about how long each note should last. This means considering **rhythm**.

The distinctive look of each note immediately tells you for how long it should be played.

A **crotchet** (or quarter note) is most often used to signify **one** beat.   *TRACK 02*

A **minim** (or half note) is worth **two** crotchet beats.   *TRACK 03*

A **semibreve** (or whole note) is worth **four** crotchet beats.   *TRACK 04*

A **quaver** (or eighth note) is worth **half** the length of a crotchet beat.   *TRACK 05*

A **semiquaver** (or sixteenth note) is worth one **quarter** of the length of a crotchet beat.   *TRACK 06*

HAVE A GO!

Try clapping the rhythms above, counting out loud as you do so. Listen to the demonstrations on the CD beforehand if you are unsure.

Time signatures

You may have noticed that the stave is divided into sections by vertical lines. These are called **barlines** and serve to divide the music into small sections called bars. The length of each **bar** is determined by the number of beats it contains and is indicated by the time signature.

The time signature of the musical examples on the previous page is 4/4.

$\frac{4}{4}$ This means that each bar is the length of **four crotchet** beats. This time signature is commonly used for music with a strong rock beat or music written in a marching style. *TRACK 07*

Two other time signatures are also very commonly used—3/4 and 6/8.

$\frac{3}{4}$ Each bar is the length of **three crotchet** beats.

A strong emphasis is often placed on the first beat of the bar when using this time signature giving the music a swaying feel. A good example of this is the waltz with its strong **1-2-3** dance rhythm. *TRACK 08*

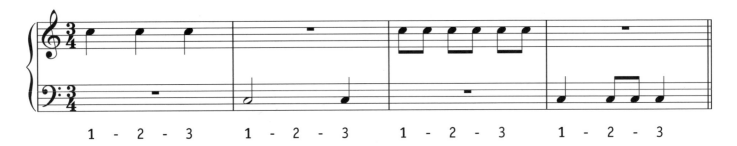

$\frac{6}{8}$ Each bar is the length of **six quaver** beats.

These quavers are grouped into two dotted crotchet beats (see explanation on page 9) giving the music a swing feel. As such it is often used in jazz and blues music. *TRACK 09*

HAVE A GO!

Try clapping the rhythms in the musical examples above in time with the CD. As you clap you will notice the different style of each time signature.

Rests and dotted notes

Knowing when not to play and how long to be silent for is just as important as knowing what notes to play and when to play them. Silence is indicated by a **rest**, and all the notes we've looked at have an equivalent rest.

A **crotchet** (or quarter note) rest is most often used to signify **one** beat.

A **minim** (or half note) rest is worth **two** crotchet beats.

A **semibreve** (or whole note) rest is worth **four** crotchet beats.

A **quaver** (or eighth note) rest is worth **half** the length of a crotchet beat.

A **semiquaver** (or sixteenth note) rest is worth one **quarter** of the length of a crotchet beat.

The length of both notes and rests can be increased by an additional 50% by writing a **dot** to the right of the note.

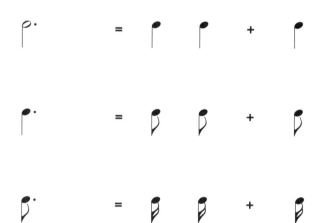

Dotted notes and rests are often used in conjunction with one another as illustrated below.   *TRACK 10*

HAVE A GO!

Try clapping the rhythm above. Take it very slowly and sub-divide the beat as you count in your head. Use the CD to check whether you are clapping the rhythms correctly.

Ties

We now know that notated music is divided into bars each containing a set number of beats. However, sometimes the composer wants a note to last for longer than the total length of one bar. In such an instance a tie is used to join two or more notes together.

In the example below four semibreves (whole notes) have been tied together. Each semibreve lasts four crotchet beats so the total note length is 16 crotchet beats.

1 - 2 - 3 - 4   1 - 2 - 3 - 4   1 - 2 - 3 - 4   1 - 2 - 3 - 4

Ties can also be used to join notes of different lengths as demonstrated below. How many beats do the tied notes last in the next example? (Turn to page 47 for the solution.)

1 - 2 - 3 - 4   1 - 2 - 3 - 4   1 - 2 - 3 - 4   1 - 2 - 3 - 4

Tied notes can also be used within a bar rather than across bars.

Here are some more examples: **TRACK 11**

1 - 2 - 3 - 4   1 - 2 - 3 - 4   1 - 2 - 3 - 4   1 - 2 - 3 - 4

1 - 2 - 3 - 4   1 - 2 - 3 - 4   1 - 2 - 3 - 4   1 - 2 - 3 - 4

HAVE A GO!

Music containing lots of tied notes is often referred to as having a **syncopated** rhythm. Clap the rhythms above, counting **1-2-3-4** throughout to help you get it right, and remember to listen to the demonstration on the CD.

Fingering

So far we have thought about notes on the piano keyboard, rhythms and time signatures.
Now it's time to get down to some actual playing using both your right and left hands.

Obviously there are far more keys on the piano than you have fingers and as such it is important to use
your fingers wisely. To help us do this we assign the fingers of each hand a number as shown below:

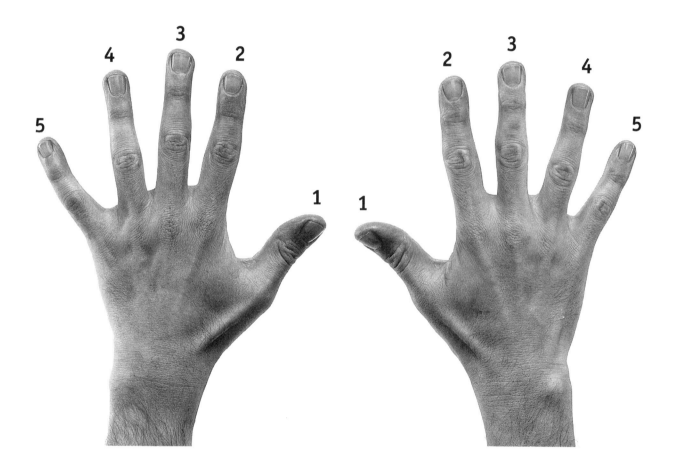

When you see a number printed above a note on the treble clef, or below a note on the bass clef,
it is telling you what finger to use to play the note.

It may feel like yet another thing to think about, but following the prescribed fingering will help you to play
the correct notes, especially as we move towards playing chords later on in this book.

As you progress as a pianist you will be able to make decisions regarding fingering yourself, but for now
follow the fingering indicated on the music.

Fingering – Right hand

Place your right-hand thumb on middle C and rest each of your four other right-hand fingers on D, E, F and G respectively. You should be covering five consecutive notes; a comfortable hand position.

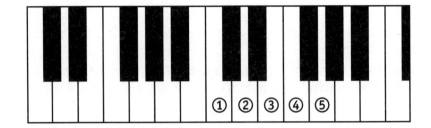

Play the exercises below following the prescribed fingering.

Exercise 1   TRACK 12
Remember to keep your fingers curved, using the pads of the fingers to play each note.
Count out loud if you want you.

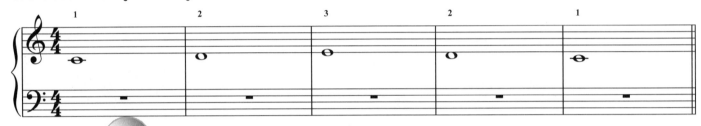

Exercise 2   TRACK 13
Try to join the end of each note to the beginning of the next, creating a smooth melodic line.

Exercise 3   TRACK 14
At first you may have to put in more effort to play the higher notes as your fourth and fifth fingers will be weaker than you thumb and first finger. With practice these will become stronger.

Exercise 4   TRACK 15
Only the first note in this exercise has fingering indicated. Keep your hand in the position detailed above with the thumb on middle C and play each key using the finger resting on it. If your hand is in the correct position it should be obvious which fingers to use.

Fingering – Left hand

Now place your left-hand thumb on middle C and rest each of your four other left-hand fingers on B, A, G and F respectively. Again, this should be a comfortable hand position with no need to stretch.

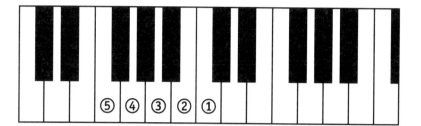

Try the following exercises adhering to the fingering recommended.

Exercise 5 *TRACK 16*
Say the letter name of each note as you play it to reinforce your new knowledge.

Exercise 6 *TRACK 17*
If you are naturally right-handed you will probably find that your left hand is much weaker than your right hand. The more you practise, the less apparent this will become.

Exercise 7 *TRACK 18*
Keep to a steady tempo, using a metronome if you need to.

Exercise 8 *TRACK 19*
Once again the fingering has been removed. If you keep your hand in the same position as used in the previous three exercises things should start to fall into place.

Fingering - Hands together

The following pieces have been written as exercises to build towards playing with both hands at the same time—'hands together'.

Exercise 9   TRACK 20
The first exercise starts on middle C in both the right hand and the left hand, and as such the thumbs of each hand are required to 'share' this key. Use the same hand positions as those adopted in the previous exercises.

Exercise 10   TRACK 21
Play through the left-hand part on its own, starting with the little finger on the C below middle C as indicated and following the prescribed fingering. Then try putting the two hands together.
(You should recognise the right-hand part from Exercise 4.)

Exercise 11   TRACK 22
This time play through the right-hand part in advance of attempting this exercise hands together. Start with your thumb on middle C and follow the recommended fingering. Then try putting the two hands together.
(You should recognise the left-hand part from Exercise 8.)

Here are three pieces that will enable you to practise playing 'hands together'.

Before playing each piece look at the time signature and check that you understand what this means.
Then clap through the rhythm in each hand, counting out loud and sub-dividing the beat if this helps you.

Position both the right and left hands according to the fingering indicated and play through each individually before putting the two together, taking it very slowly at first.

The first piece is a short extract from a classical piece of music that you may recognise thanks to its extensive use in TV advertising. The second is another anthemic classical work, and the third a pop song that has also made its way onto stage and screen.

Excerpt from 'Largo' (from 'From The New World Symphony') TRACK 23
Music by Antonin Dvořák

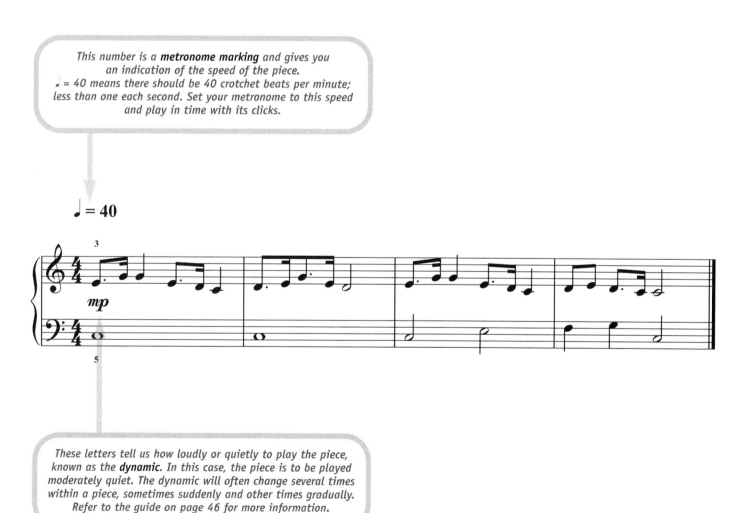

This number is a **metronome marking** and gives you an indication of the speed of the piece.
♩ = 40 means there should be 40 crotchet beats per minute; less than one each second. Set your metronome to this speed and play in time with its clicks.

These letters tell us how loudly or quietly to play the piece, known as the **dynamic**. In this case, the piece is to be played moderately quiet. The dynamic will often change several times within a piece, sometimes suddenly and other times gradually. Refer to the guide on page 46 for more information.

Ode To Joy

(from 'Symphony No.9')

Music by Ludwig van Beethoven

This is the main theme from the last movement of Beethoven's ninth and final symphony. It took six years to complete and by the time the première was given in 1823 the composer was completely deaf.

*The number at the far left-hand edge of each line is the **bar number**. This is often a useful reference point.*

*This text tells you the **style** in which to play the piece, in this case, 'stately'.*

Stately ♩ = 112

Mamma Mia

Words & Music by Benny Andersson, Stig Anderson & Björn Ulvaeus

The song that two decades later lent its name to the international smash Abba musical first came out in 1975. Anyone wanting to know what makes a great pop song need only listen to this sublime demonstration.

This curved line is a **slur**. When two notes are linked together using a slur you should endeavour to move from one to another as smoothly as possible. It is commonly used when a syllable (or one-syllable word) is spread over two or more notes.

The **lyrics** are included so you can sing as well as play the piano, although you probably need to master the music first. Reading through the words might also help you with the rhythm.

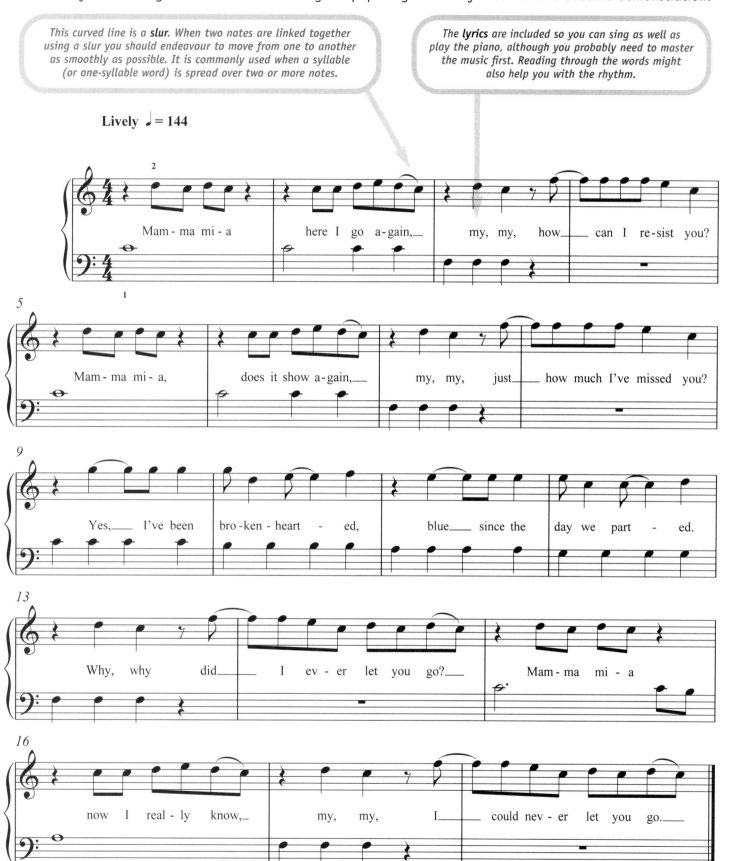

Lively ♩ = 144

Mam - ma mi - a here I go a - gain,__ my, my, how__ can I re-sist you?

Mam - ma mi - a, does it show a - gain,__ my, my, just__ how much I've missed you?

Yes,__ I've been bro - ken - heart - ed, blue__ since the day we part - ed.

Why, why did__ I ev - er let you go?__ Mam - ma mi - a

now I real - ly know,__ my, my, I__ could nev - er let you go.__

Shifting position – Right hand

So far our hands have not had to shift their positioning on the piano keyboard within a piece, but this will not always be the case. In order to play a wider range of notes you will need to move your hand up and down the keys.

Try the exercises below, following the recommended fingering throughout. This is where the fingering indications become particularly helpful!

Exercise 12   TRACK 26
Start with your thumb on middle C and your hand in the position used in the previous right-hand exercises, such that your five fingers span keys C–G.

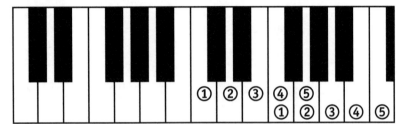

As you approach the first beat of the second bar, slot your thumb underneath your other fingers and place it on F.
As you play this note, reposition your fingers such that they are spanning keys F–C and continue.

As you approach the first note of the last bar, cross your third finger over your thumb and place it on E.
As you play this note, reposition your thumb and index finger over the keys C and D and continue.

Play this exercise through a number of times, until you can transition smoothly between the different hand positions. Count a slow **1-2-3-4** before starting to play and keep counting as you play.

Exercise 13   TRACK 27
Start with your thumb on F, such that your five fingers span keys F–C.

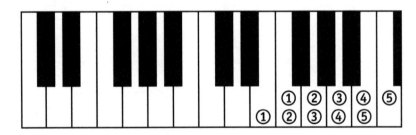

Half-way through the second bar reposition your hand, putting your fourth finger on A, such that your five fingers span keys E–B, one key lower than the initial hand position.

Half-way through the third bar reposition your hand putting your index finger on G, such that your five fingers span keys F–C, reverting to the original hand position.

Shifting position – Left hand

Let's try exercises along a similar vein to these but in the left hand.

Exercise 14   TRACK 28

Start with your thumb on middle C and your hand in the position used in the previous left-hand exercises, such that your five fingers span keys F–C.

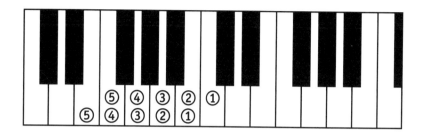

> *As you approach the first beat of the second bar, move your index finger down the keyboard and place it on A. As you play this note, reposition your fingers such that you are spanning keys E–B, one key lower than your original hand position.*

> *As you approach the first note of the third bar, stretch your fourth finger and place it on G. As you play this note, reposition your fingers such that you are spanning keys F–C, as per the original hand position.*

Exercise 15   TRACK 29

Start with your thumb on middle C and your hand in the position used in the previous left-hand exercises, such that your five fingers span keys F–C.

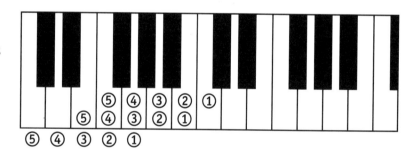

> *As you approach the first beat of the second bar, move your index finger down the keyboard and place it on A. As you play this note, reposition your fingers such that you are spanning keys E–B, one key lower that your original hand position.*

> *As you approach the first note of the third bar, move your thumb down the keyboard and place it on G. As you play this note, reposition your fingers such that you are spanning keys C–G, with your little finger on the C below middle C.*

Shifting position – Hands together

Exercise 16   *TRACK 30*

Try combining shifting the position of the right hand with a simple left-hand accompaniment.
You should recognise the right-hand part from previous exercises.

Exercise 17   *TRACK 31*

Try combining shifting the position of the left hand with a simple right-hand accompaniment.
Likewise, you should recognise the left-hand part from previous exercises.

On the next three pages are pieces that will enable you to practise shifting your hand positions.
Pay careful attention to the fingering.

I Walk The Line

Words & Music by Johnny Cash

The chronicle of the life of country-music legend Johnny Cash, from his upbringing on an Arkansas cotton farm to a recording career with Sun Records in Memphis, took its title from this, his first No. 1 hit.

> The right hand must move up the keyboard at bar 11 and back down the keyboard at bar 13. The left hand can remain in the same position throughout the piece.

> This symbol, an **accent**, indicates that the note should be played with extra weight. Exert greater force on the keys with both hands as you play the last note.

Country ♩ = 108

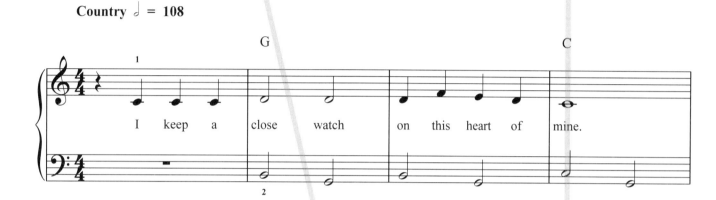

I keep a close watch on this heart of mine.

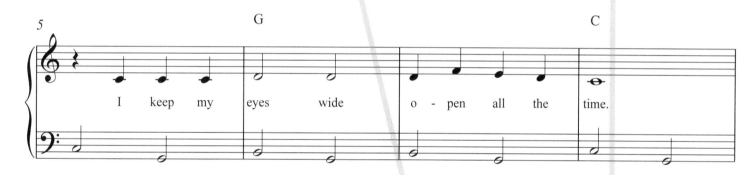

I keep my eyes wide open all the time.

I keep the ends out for the tie that binds,

be - cause you're mine, I walk the line.

Largo

(from 'From The New World Symphony')

Music by Antonín Dvořák

Dvořák, a Czech composer, composed this piece whilst living in the USA. It uses themes, although entirely original, inspired by African-American traditional melodies.

Shift your right hand up the keyboard such that your third finger is on A at this point. Your hand will remain in this position until bar 9 when it moves back to its original position.

Swan Lake

Music by Pyotr Ilyich Tchaikovsky

This famous theme from the ballet of the same name was composed by the Russian composer Tchaikovsky.
The motif (or scène) appears in several different guises throughout the piece.

Stretching position

It is sometimes necessary for the five fingers on each hand not to be placed on consecutive keys.
Place your thumb on middle C and stretch your fingers as far as you can. How far can you reach?

Exercise 18   TRACK 35
Play through the following exercise very slowly, taking care over the stretch between the first and second
notes in the first and third bars. Note that the piece is in a different time signature, 3/4, and how the music
feels more like a waltz than a march.

Exercise 19   TRACK 36
Play through this exercise very slowly, taking care over the stretches in the second bar and the octave leap
between the penultimate note and last note.

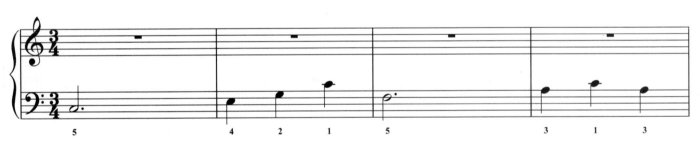

Exercise 20 *TRACK 37*

Let's try putting these two parts together.

Excerpt from 'Trumpet Voluntary' *TRACK 38*

Music by Jeremiah Clarke

This extract is often used as a trumpet fanfare at weddings. Although the right hand only shifts position once, the left hand will require your utmost concentration as it covers a much wider range of notes than your hand could reach in its usual position.

> *This dynamic marking indicates that the piece should be played 'forte' meaning 'loudly'. Refer to the guide on page 46 for more information.*

> *The dots next to the final barline are repeat markings and tell us to go back to the beginning of the piece and play it through again.*

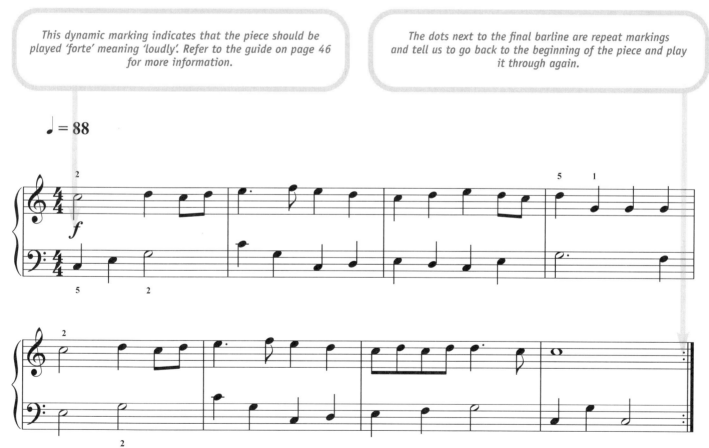

On the next page you will find an arrangement of all-time favourite 'Hallelujah' by Leonard Cohen which uses a mixture of shifting hand positions (the right hand in bar 12 and bar 16) and stretches (the right hand in bar 8 and the left hand in bar 24). The song is in 6/8; turn back to page 8 if you need to refresh your memory as to what this means.

Hallelujah

Words & Music by Leonard Cohen

First recorded, with 15 verses, by Leonard Cohen on his 1984 album *Various Positions*, and nominated by *Q Magazine* in September 2007 as the most perfect song ever, various versions of this song have featured on the soundtracks of several movies and TV shows, most often during scenes which involve death or heartbreak.

Hints & Tips: Pay careful attention to placing the right-hand and left-hand notes together, especially the last quaver beat of each bar.

26

Accidentals

You will have noticed that so far we have played only white keys of the piano. Our musical language needs to be able to tell us when to play the black keys too. Rather than label the black keys with additional letters, they are described using associated **accidentals** – **sharps** and **flats**.

♯ A sharp is to the right of the white key and sounds slightly higher than the white note sounds.

♭ A flat is to the left of the white note and sounds slightly lower than the white note sounds.

Here are some examples of sharps and flats written on the stave.

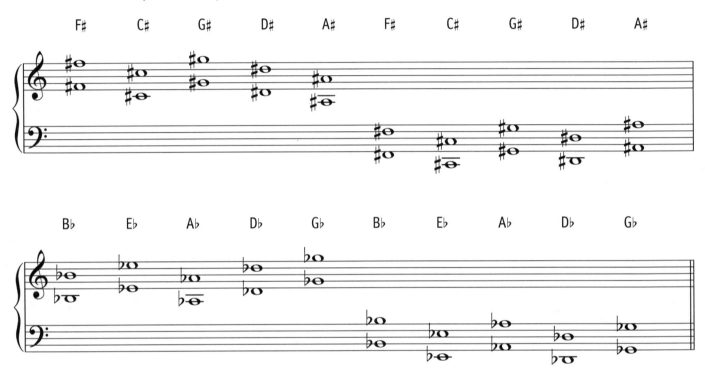

HAVE A GO!

Identify the notes below by writing the letter name of each note in the gaps. (You'll find the solution on page 47.) Then try finding the notes on the piano, checking yourself against the CD.   *TRACK 40*

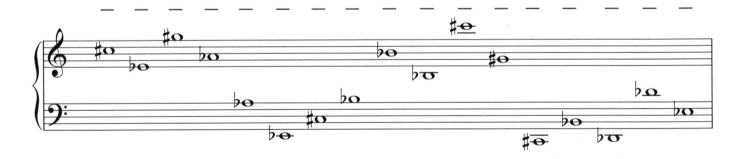

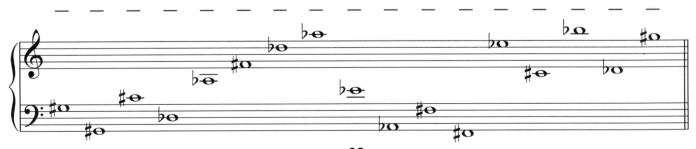

Key signatures

When a sharp or flat appears in a bar it applies to every corresponding note in that bar. However, if a sharp or flat is to be used throughout a piece, we can use a key signature.

A key signature appears at the left end of the stave and comprises zero to seven sharps or flats, although we will only look at key signatures with three or less accidentals.

The key signature dictates which black keys should be played in a piece. This means there is no need to print sharps and flats throughout the music, making it easier to read; you just need to remember to play a sharp or flat every time the corresponding note appears in the music.

Unless...

There is another symbol closely associated with sharps and flats, the natural sign, ♮.
This symbol serves to cancel any sharps or flats in the key signature and any accidentals that have appeared in the bar.

The piece on the next page, a minuet by the baroque composer J. S. Bach, has one sharp, F♯, in the key signature. Remember that this applies to every F that appears in either hand. There are also a number of accidentals in the second half of the piece so watch out for these.

The Beatles song that follows features a number of accidentals, both sharps and flats. Remember that these should apply to the entire bar in which they appear unless there is also a natural sign to cancel them out.

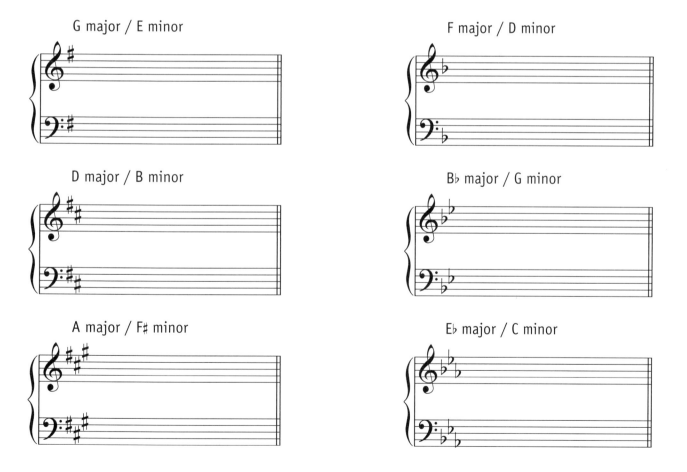

Minuet In G

(from 'Anna Magdelena Notebook')

Music by Johann Sebastian Bach

This minuet is taken from the two books of collected pieces that Bach compiled for his second wife Anna Magdalena. She was the daughter of one of the musicians in the orchestra and apparently a gifted soprano.

*The small dot underneath this note indicate that the note should be played **staccato**, meaning shortened and therefore slightly detached from both the previous and next notes. This is achieved by letting the key rise quickly after playing it, rather than holding it down with your finger.*

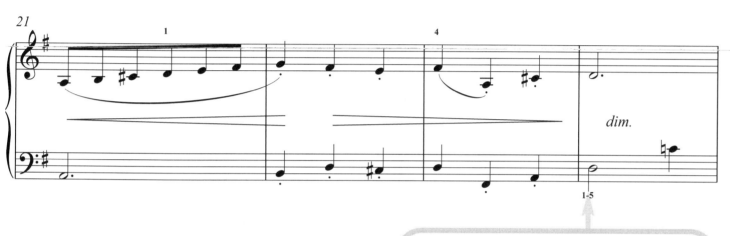

This fingering tells you to play D with your left-hand thumb, and swap onto your fifth finger whilst holding down the note, freeing up your thumb to reach up to the middle C.

From Me To You

Words & Music by John Lennon & Paul McCartney

By topping the charts for seven weeks from 2 May 1963, the Beatles' third single on the Parlophone label became the first of their 11 consecutive UK No. 1 hit singles and, sandwiched between two songs by Gerry & The Pacemakers, the second of three consecutive No. 1 hits produced by George Martin.

> *So far all the pieces we have played have started on the first beat of the bar. It is very common, however, for a tune not to start with a complete bar. The musical term for this is an **anacrusis** or **upbeat**. There is only one crotchet beat in the first bar of this example although the time signature indicates that there should be four. Count **1-2-3-4** as you would normally but start playing on the fourth beat.*

> *Watch out for both this sharpened note and the natural sign that follows it.*

Laid-back ♩ = 160

Da da da da da dum dum da. Da da da da da dum dum

da. If there's an-y-thing that you want,___ if there's

an-y-thing I can do,___ just call on me___ and I'll

send it a-long___ with love___ from me___ to you.___ I've got

Remember that this flat sign applies to all the Bs in this bar.

Chords

So far our musical examples have featured both the right and left hands, sometimes playing 'hands together', but with each hand playing only one note. The music we play will sound far more interesting if we are able to play more than one note in each hand at one time. As such the time has come to get our minds and fingers working a little harder as we start to play **chords**.

A **chord** is two or more notes played simultaneously. It is therefore very important to use the best fingering.

HAVE A GO!

Use these simple pieces as exercises. Take them very slowly and remember to read the fingering.

Exercise 21   *TRACK 43*
Let's start with the right hand.

Exercise 22   *TRACK 44*
Next up is the left hand.

Exercise 23   *TRACK 45*
Now we're ready for some slightly more difficult progressions.

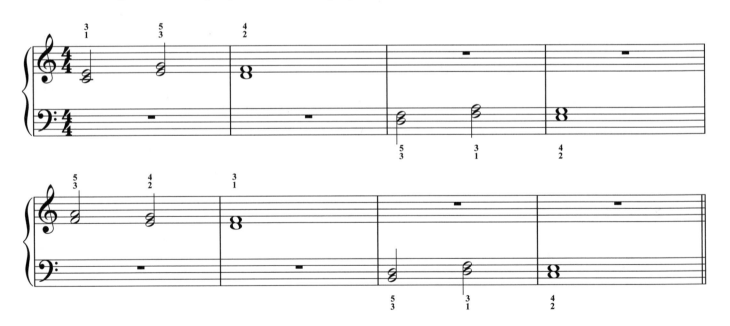

So far all the chords you have played have contained a maximum of two notes in one hand but you've got five fingers on each hand so let's try some three-note chords!

Exercise 24   TRACK 46

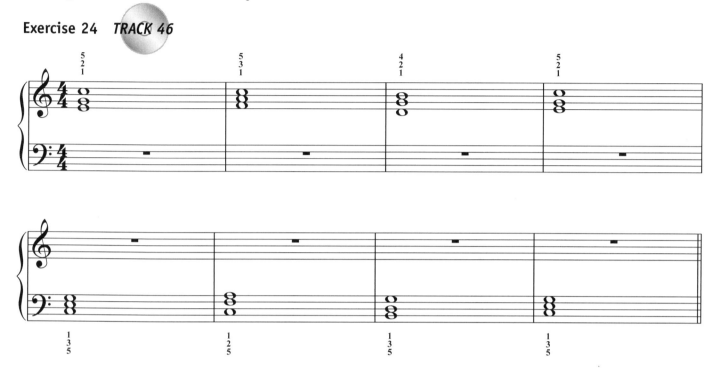

A chord is very often used as an accompaniment to a melody as demonstrated in this next example.

Exercise 25   TRACK 47

There are a number of other ways the left hand can be used to accompany a melody, each synonymous with a different style. On the following pages you will find several pieces of music, both classical and contemporary, each representing a different musical genre. Different time signatures, rhythms, dynamics and accents also contribute to the distinct sound of each piece.

The Blue Danube

Music by Johann Strauss II

This piece is a **waltz**, a dance in 3/4 time. From Strauss, a master of the waltz, to *Strictly Come Dancing*, this dance has been enjoyed for over 200 years.

> The lilt of the waltz is created by placing an emphasis on the first beat of each bar, 1-2-3, and keeping the second and third beats in the left hand very light.

> The right hand jumps about the piano keyboard but don't leave these movements to the last minute. Instead, look ahead, and move your hand to the correct position in the rests.

Waltz ♩ = 156

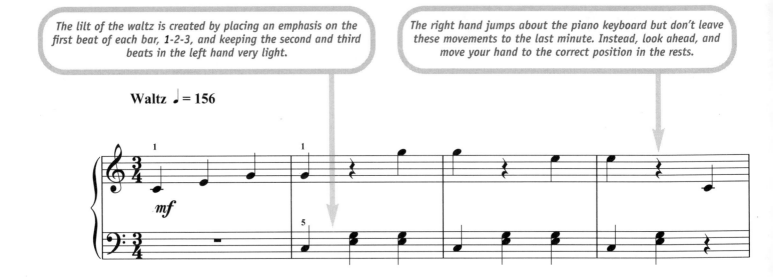

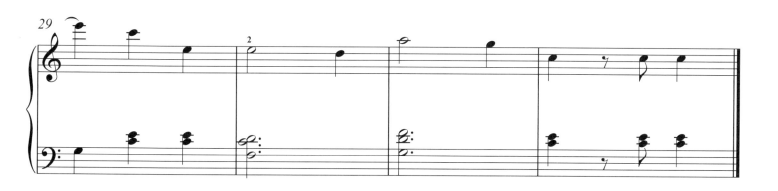

Clarinet Concerto

(Theme)

Music by Wolfgang Amadeus Mozart

Although this piece is also in 3/4 time, it has a very different feel to the waltz; the music is very much led by the melody rather than driven by the rhythm of the accompaniment.

Listen carefully as you play the chords in the left hand to ensure the two notes are sounding at the same time.

*These long curved lines indicate the phrasing of the music. A musical **phrase** is equivalent to a sentence in speech. Try to join the notes within a phrase as smoothly as possible and take time to 'breath' between the phrases.*

Morning

(from 'Peer Gynt')

Music by Edvard Grieg

This work is one of a series of incidental pieces Grieg wrote for Henrik Ibsen's play *Peer Gynt*.
Written in 6/8, it should be played with a strong sense of two dotted crotchet beats in each bar (rather than
three crotchet beats as per the last two pieces).

Remember an accidental lasts right through the bar.

*Try to achieve the transitions between the different hand
positions required as smoothly as possible.*

In two ♩. = 56

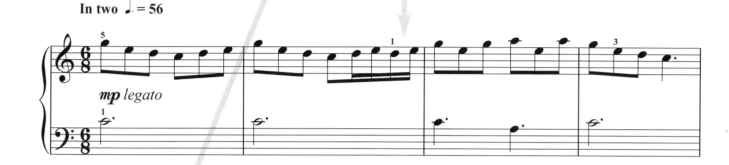

Yellow

Words & Music by Guy Berryman, Chris Martin, Jon Buckland & Will Champion

'Yellow' became the breakthrough single for British pop/rock band Coldplay when it shot to No. 4 in the UK singles chart. It is a great example of a **slow rock** song—a strong sense of pulse is created by the left hand providing a simple bass-line accompaniment to a repetitive, plaintive melody.

> *The left hand should be played lightly and more softly than the right hand. However, placing a slight emphasis on the first quaver of each bar will avoid the accompaniment sounding monotonous.*

> *These letters are **chord symbols**. If you know someone that plays the guitar, you could ask them to strum along to the piece as you play it using these letters to tell them what chords to play.*

Slow rock ♩ = 86

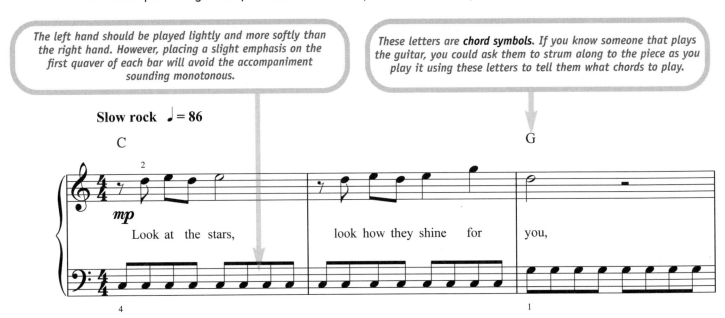

Look at the stars, look how they shine for you,

and ev'ry-thing you do. Yeah, they were all yel-low. I came a-long,

I wrote a song for you, and all the things you do.

Mrs Robinson

Words & Music by Paul Simon

This song, by one half of the legendary duo Simon & Garfunkel, was written for the film *The Graduate*. Unlike the previous pieces, the chords are in the right hand, whilst the left hand bounces between notes to form a bass-line. These chords represent the two voices on the original **pop** record.

There are a number of new symbols on this music which indicate the structure of the song. Look ahead to bar 38 and notice that the music stops abruptly. The text 'D.S.' stands for 'dal segno' and tells you to return to this symbol.

Play through the music for a second time until you reach this point. Then follow the instruction to jump 'To Coda'. The coda is the extra section at the end of the piece, in this case just one bar, and creates an ending to the song.

Triplets

Before you play the last piece in the book, there is one last element of rhythm to introduce, the triplet.

A **triplet** is a group of three notes, equal in length, which are to be fitted into the time that two notes of the same type would take. It is indicated on the musical score by using a small '3' over or under the notes as shown below.

   These three minims are to be played in the time of two minims (equal to one semibreve).

   These three crotchets are to be played in the time of two crotchets (equal to one minum).

These three quavers are to be played in the time of two quavers (equal to one crotchet).

These three semiquavers are to be played in the time of two semiquavers (equal to one quaver).

HAVE A GO!

This is easier to play than to describe so try this simple exercise which features various triplets.
Clap the rhythm first counting **1-2-3-4** as you go.

Exercise 26   TRACK 53

Triplet rhythms are also used, particularly in **jazz** and **blues** music, to create a **swing** feel.
Often this is indicated at the beginning of the piece using the following annotation.

Listen to the demonstration of the song on the next page, 'I Believe', which uses this swing indication to understand how this rhythm sounds.

I Believe

Words & Music by Ervin Drake, Irvin Graham, Jimmy Shirl & Al Stillman

This pop ballad with a swing feel has reached the top of the UK charts four times and holds the record for the most weeks spent at No. 1. Frankie Laine's original topped the charts on three separate occasions in 1953, and over 40 years later Robson & Jerome reached No. 1 with their cover version.

Play this song with a swing feel by making the first quaver in each pair slightly longer than the second.

Although not indicated, introduce dynamics to your performance to heighten the sense of emotion.

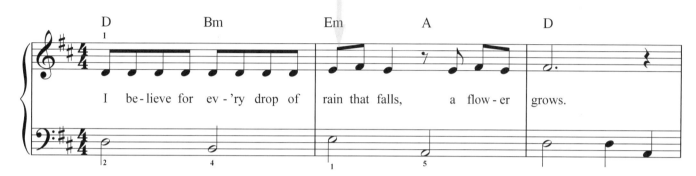

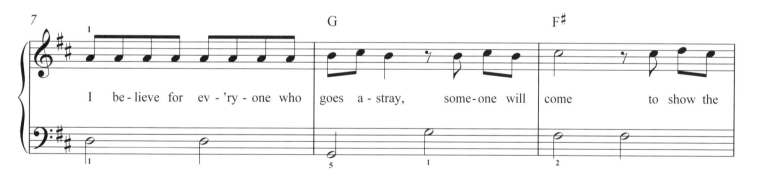

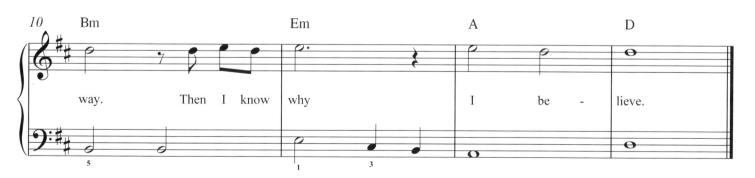

Dynamics, tempo & style glossary

Whilst you may now be able to recognise what notes to play, when to play them and how long to play them for, another aspect of your performance that the composer or songwriter may want to communicate to you is how you play the notes.

For example, should the piece be played loudly or quietly, at a fast pace or slowly? To indicate this a real language, Italian, is often used, as well as abbreviations and symbols.

Dynamics

pianissimo or *pp* = very soft

piano or *p* = soft

mezzo piano or *mp* = medium soft

mezzo forte or *mf* = medium loud

forte or *f* = loud

fortissimo or *ff* = very loud

diminuendo (or dim.) or
 = gradually get quieter

crescendo (or cresc.) or
= gradually get louder

Tempo

Largo = very slow

Adagio = slow

Andante = walking pace

Moderato = moderately fast

Allegro = fast

Presto = very fast

rallentando (or rall.) = gradually get slower

accelerando (or accel.) = gradually get faster

Style

In addition to dynamics and tempo, the composer or songwriter may want to dictate a particular style in which the piece, or individual notes within the piece, should be played. A march, for example, should be played boldly and perhaps aggressively; the notes detached from one another. Whereas a lullaby should be played gently, moving from each note to the next as smoothly as possible. Once again various Italian terms are used to indicate this.

Legato = smooth, flowing style
Staccato = short, clipped notes

Solutions

Making the connection (page 6)

C E G A A E C B B B C G C B D D E

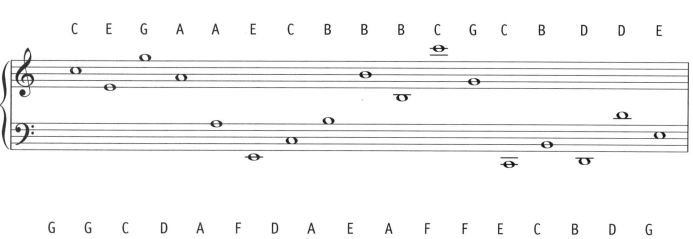

G G C D A F D A E A F F E C B D G

Ties (page 10)

= 1+1/2 crotchet beats   = 3 crotchet beats   = 1 crotchet beat

Accidentals (page 28)

C# Eb G# Ab Ab Eb C# Bb Bb Bb C# G# C# Bb Db Db Eb

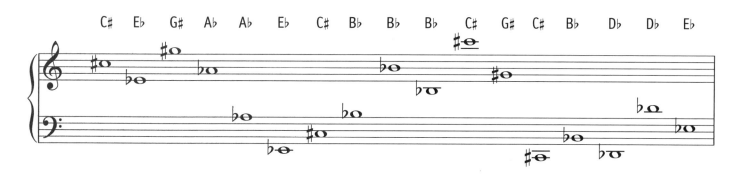

G# G# C# Db Ab F# Db Ab Eb Ab F# F# Eb C# Bb Db G#

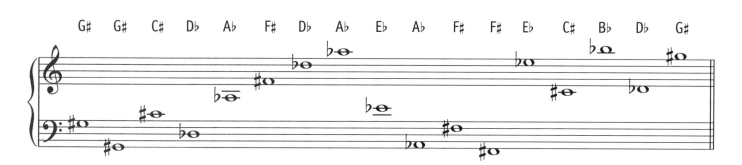

47

CD tracklisting

01 Making the connection

02 Rhythm – Crotchets

03 Rhythm – Minims

04 Rhythm – Semibreves

05 Rhythm – Quavers

06 Rhythm – Semiquavers

07 Time signatures – 4/4

08 Time signatures – 3/4

09 Time signatures – 6/8

10 Rests and dotted notes

11 Ties

12 Exercise 1

13 Exercise 2

14 Exercise 3

15 Exercise 4

16 Exercise 5

17 Exercise 6

18 Exercise 7

19 Exercise 8

20 Exercise 9

21 Exercise 10

22 Exercise 11

23 Largo (excerpt)
(Dvořák)
Dorsey Brothers Music Limited.

24 Ode To Joy
(Beethoven)
Dorsey Brothers Music Limited.

25 Mamma Mia
(Andersson/Anderson/Ulvaeus)
Bocu Music Limited.

26 Exercise 12

27 Exercise 13

28 Exercise 14

29 Exercise 15

30 Exercise 16

31 Exercise 17

32 I Walk The Line
(Cash)
Carlin Music Corporation.

33 Largo
(Dvořák)
Dorsey Brothers Music Limited.

34 Swan Lake (Theme)
(Tchaikovsky)
Dorsey Brothers Music Limited.

35 Exercise 18

36 Exercise 19

37 Exercise 20

38 Trumpet Voluntary (excerpt)
(Clarke)
Dorsey Brothers Music Limited.

39 Hallelujah
(Cohen)
Sony/ATV Music Publishing (UK) Limited.

40 Accidentals

41 Minuet In G
(Bach)
Dorsey Brothers Music Limited.

42 From Me To You
(Lennon/McCartney)
Sony/ATV Music Publishing (UK) Limited.

43 Exercise 21

44 Exercise 22

45 Exercise 23

46 Exercise 24

47 Exercise 25

48 The Blue Danube
(Strauss)
Dorsey Brothers Music Limited.

49 Clarinet Concerto (Theme)
(Mozart)
Dorsey Brothers Music Limited.

50 Morning
(Grieg)
Dorsey Brothers Music Limited.

51 Yellow
(Berryman/Martin/Buckland/Champion)
Universal Music Publishing MGB Limited.

52 Mrs Robinson
(Simon)
Universal/MCA Music Limited.

53 Exercise 26

54 I Believe
(Drake/Graham/Shirl/Stillman)
TRO Essex Music Limited.

3 4 5 6 7 8 9